Edge of Highway

Poems

J. A. Lagana

Finishing Line Press
Georgetown, Kentucky

Edge of Highway

Copyright © 2025 by J. A. Lagana
ISBN 979-8-88838-966-9 First Edition
All rights reserved under International and Pan-American Copyright Conventions. No part of this book may be reproduced in any manner whatsoever without written permission from the publisher, except in the case of brief quotations embodied in critical articles and reviews.

ACKNOWLEDGMENTS

Many thanks to the editors of the following publications in which earlier or current versions of these poems have appeared or are forthcoming:

Amethyst Review: "Eastbound"
RockPaperPoem: "The sky held odd and white for days after" which appears as "Remnants"
San Antonio Review: "Respite"; "U-turn"; "Yield"
The engine(idling: "Night"
Thimble: "Detour"
US#1 Worksheets: "Exit"

Love and thanks to my husband, Tony Lagana, for his consistent encouragement.

Thank you to my friends in the NJ and PA poetry communities for your uplifting conversations about writing, creativity, and life.

Special shout out to the members of the New Hope Poets and Writers group for considering several of these poems in their earliest forms.

To all the commuters making the long, daily round-trip drive, stay safe and enjoy the ride.

Publisher: Leah Huete de Maines
Editor: Christen Kincaid
Cover Art: Michael James
Author Photo: Tony Lagana
Cover Design: Elizabeth Maines McCleavy

Order online: www.finishinglinepress.com
also available on amazon.com

Author inquiries and mail orders:
Finishing Line Press
PO Box 1626
Georgetown, Kentucky 40324
USA

Contents

Eastbound 1

Drive 2

Field 3

Curve 4

Traffic 5

Lost 6

Respite 7

Lift 8

Roadside 9

Yield 10

Detour 11

Coryell 12

Exit 13

Remnants 14

Direction 15

Night 16

U-Turn 17

For Tony

Eastbound

Slick lanes, moonlit.
White lines, rhinestoned.
    Another mile or two to go.
    The drive made bearable
by the incremental presence
    of street lamps.
Silver-tipped,
they line the route,
high as treetops
from some sacred place.
Pensive metal,
their top-caps
and cameras,
dusted in snow.

Drive

The steadiness of traffic
clears the head, brakes anxiety,
                offers second chances.
Woosh, woosh. The quick pace.
The rush to be somewhere else.

Four lanes fold into three.
Fog-misted exit signs
reveal themselves
like muddled spirits
at play with the truth.

Field

Dawn and sparrows lift
    along this edge of highway
like blankets strewn
    across a lover's bed.

Ahead,
the sense to yield, ignored.

Rough road. Swoop of blackbirds against a spate
of orange clouds.
        Work and home
off-kilter. Desires
that won't break down.

    The cues to merge
mere warning signs.

Curve

Twice-a-day the same route,
leave-taking and back.
      Bluetoothed conversations
  and before the next exit
the phone again
with another misunderstanding—
    as if a random singer
joined the ride, insistent
on the usual
  lyrical repeats,
indifferent
  to how a fresh rhythm
or new turn
might improve the old song.

Traffic

Their figures shadowed
by the tail lights' glow,
the highway road crew
waves us through.
    Move on, move on.

Their voices rise as they point us
toward a detour. This less-familiar route,
full of promise
like our last half-hearted phone call.
    Move on, move on.

Traffic's stalled.
No one's moving forward.

Lost

The unexpected downpour.
Thunder claps and construction cones.
Barns and fields a-smudge.

Tire-raps over gravel.

The phone's repeated buzz
as if an out-of-season bug,
caught in its last throes,
still vied for attention.

Harsh words.
The car's wipers, furious.

What chance is there, ever,
to halt desire's forward momentum?

Rush of brake lights.
Another strike like a crescendo
after the pitch turns.

The electrically charged sky.
The quiescent aftermath.

Our silence was everything.
It held all we couldn't say.

Birds, hushed. The wind's swell.

Respite

The vibrancy in that small cafe
all of us concerned mostly
about breakfast.
        Around the corner
        wide sky for miles.
The land, yellow-brown and hard
and being city folk from the suburbs
        we were silenced.
We spotted the familiar from the road.
Wild sage. Coneflowers.
Cheatgrass.
Saw black-chinned hummingbirds
        and a skyline
of sandstone cliff shadows
huddled
as if in conversation, prayer,
or the something deeper
        we were seeking.
        At the Narrows water flowed
above our hips. Our feet arched
over river rocks, uncertain
        as rain clouds.
        Later, we lay
side-by-side, backs against a boulder,
        got lost in the spaces
between stars
        that stared back,
raised questions,
        understood
we were too overcome
to reply.

Lift

Road-side flocks
claw a dead season's fields

as ravenous as lovers
after a dry spell.

Spent ground. A fling of stalks,
                            feathers,
                  tumble, tumble,
    t
      u m
             b
   l
     e.

Roadside

Brake lights flash
with urgency
      as if the turn
        of another season
can't come fast enough.

Patches of freeway daisies blur
along the slow lane's edge.

Roadside petals scatter.

      Most fail to keep
their muted holds.

Fleeting blossoms.

      For weeks they keep until,
until,
    until.

Tonight's sky, streaked slate.
    Traffic's steady.
    The entirety of you, faded.
Sans fear, sans pain.
Elsewhere.

Yield

Under the triple-laned lit-up
turnpike overpass
sharp-tipped weeds reach up
through weathered rocks, unaware
of how hard someone
tried to stop them.
There is growth under everything.

Beyond the WaWa, those bagel shops,
the Costco station that opens at 6AM,
familiar curls of highway
gleam in the pre-dawn,
and on the radio, a slow jazz movement
after the DJ's promise
that an upcoming interview
may offer a glimpse
into a better way.

Upturned orange detour signs
rest on weedy guardrails.
In the rear-view, a line of cars in wait.
The red light lingers and in the lull,
predictability is comfort. Will you consider
how easy it is then, to start anew
once the light turns?

      The traffic, on the move again.
Its cadence quickens, then slows. Quickens.
Then slows.

Detour

Snow-weighted branches
      skim the car's roof
          with a fade
and groove as if a waning beat
could signal closure and we'd be
done for good with things.
I loved you most in winter.
          That hum
    of sleet and tires.
      The uncertainties of ice
and a narrow road.
        The phone's bad connection.
        Your voice breaking up.

Coryell

Swirling over street tree branches
and rowhouse rooftops, a kettle

of turkey vultures. Their numbers
could mean luck or at least a break

in tension. Day breaks
above the pair of folding chairs

a neighbor placed to mark
a snow-cleared parking space.

The attempt to set boundaries,
admirable. The streets slushed gray.

A line of cars on Bridge Street.
A plow plods through

as tentatively as the way
in which we engage

these days. Perhaps there's a lesson
in this slow go of a morning.

The patience it requires
to hold silence

and allow time to work its way.
The traffic, headed out of town.

The birds, in committee now,
sulk, stare, keep their wings close,

await the sun's full expression,
certain it will come.

Exit

The highway's four lanes.
    Someone at the cross-walk in a red scarf and parka
    de-lids a coffee cup, frees swirls of steam
as if trying to conjure up a genie.

If you had one wish,
    what would it be?

The ice weighs upon what was once vibrant.
    Some branches break,
lost in a ramble beyond the rails.
Others beautify the drive.

Our past packaged, neat—
like stacks of albums
trunked away.

The snow, marbled, piled high.
Most mornings, it's tough
to make the light.

Remnants

The sky held odd and white
for days after
as you slipped
between the river birch branches
and wineberry shrubs along the drive.
Your breath,
gone elsewhere
while the morning's mist stayed.
      That week, even the dog
remained indifferent.
A pair of disbelievers, he and I.

The crows pause nightly now on the water tower,
      the wineberries, weighted down—
their fat orbs as somber as a glow of tail lights,
passing strands of sparkle that float
and fade along the roadway's
pebbled edge.

Some days, if the way is clear,
I'll forget basic truths
and focus on the blanketed horses
clustered near the bend.
      You,
          part of a past life now,
          are a bird glimpsed in the rear view.
      That last time,
we laughed over our waitress's good sense
      to pour more coffee,
      which allowed more time to talk.
The diner open all night.
If we could sit together
again, I'd take slower sips,
ask you more questions,
encourage you to stay.

Direction

Traffic snarls. A cardinal peeks out
on this furtive road as if in search
    of a reprieve
from warped branches. Entanglements.

    Flutters of red-winged blackbirds
over the next mile. The drive to nest
in weed beds, instinctive,
like a guilty party's last chance effort
to re-establish inner-harmony.

    The car's windows rolled tight.
Chortles of birdsong. Cacophonies
of sparrows, hawks and jays.
A hullaballoo of joy
and relief come through
and yes, I'll untangle the mess I've made,
    maybe learn to avoid
the troublesome lanes.

Night

i.
With the top down
echoes of fox cries.
   Wing flaps.
Low-flying geese.

ii.
Breezes pull placidly
over sweet potato acres.
Corn stalks a-shuffle. It's a joy
to be off the Interstate.

iii.
Beyond the barn
along the river,
   evening's
first star.

iv.
The dashboard lights
line up like Orion.
   Proof there's beauty
   everywhere.

v.
A crescent moon
tipped so low against the field
that I still regret
not risking
a second glance.
If you want the truth,
   the deer were running.

U-Turn

Nothing more
than a glimpse
of another white-bellied
cooper hawk
high at rest
      along the interstate
on a no-traffic evening.
      That feel of heading home
as if nothing
had ever happened. Oh, forgiveness
and understanding. Let us say
grace. Let us
call it that.
      Now, together.

For over two decades, writer **J. A. Lagana** drove three-hours round-trip, five days per week, on her daily commute. Her poems have appeared in *Atlanta Review, Burningword Literary Journal, Cider Press Review, Heron Tree, Rattle, RockPaperPoem,* and elsewhere. She is the author of the poetry collection *Make Space* (Finishing Line Press, 2023) which explores the complexities of loss, family ties, and resiliency. A finalist for the 2023 Julia Peterkin Award in Poetry, she is also a founder and former co-editor of *River Heron Review*. J. A. Lagana lives in a Bucks County, Pennsylvania river town where she raised a family with her husband, Tony. Learn more at jlagana.com.
https://www.jlagana.com

www.ingramcontent.com/pod-product-compliance
Lightning Source LLC
Chambersburg PA
CBHW030053100426
42734CB00038B/1539